Wandering &
Wondering

Wandering & Wondering

KENNETH V. BROWN

MORNING JOY MEDIA
POTTSTOWN, PENNSYLVANIA

Published by Morning Joy Media.

Visit morningjoymedia.com for more information on bulk discounts and special promotions, or e-mail your questions to info@morningjoymedia.com.

All Scripture quotations, unless otherwise indicated, are taken from the Holy Bible, New International Version®, NIV®. Copyright ©1973, 1978, 1984, 2011 by Biblica, Inc.™ Used by permission of Zondervan. All rights reserved worldwide. www.zondervan.com. The "NIV" and "New International Version" are trademarks registered in the United States Patent and Trademark Office by Biblica, Inc.™

Scriptures marked KJV are taken from the KING JAMES VERSION (KJV): KING JAMES VERSION, public domain.

Kenneth Brown & Family Photos: provided by the Estate of Kenneth V. Brown
Design: Debbie Capeci
Cover Images: Adobe Stock

Brown, Kenneth V.
Wandering & Wondering / by Kenneth V. Brown.

Summary: A posthumous publication of the writings of Rev. Kenneth V. Brown, who for many years was a Presbyterian pastor. The author shares reflections upon his life in the Norristown, Pennsylvania, area, and connects his musings to God's sovereinty and benevolence over our lives.

RELIGION / Christian Living / Personal Memoirs
RELIGION / Christian Living / Devotional
RELIGION / Christianity / Presbyterian

ISBN 978-1-937107-81-9 (paperback)
ISBN 978-1-937107-82-6 (ebook)

Printed in the United States of America

Dedicated to my Lord Jesus Christ
    Who called me to this walk of faith
    And walked it with me.
And to my wife, Anne,
    Who patiently endured my wanderings
    And lovingly comforted me in the way.

—The Rev. Kenneth V. Brown

Contents

Preface

AFTER MY DAD'S PASSING IN May of 2009 there was a mountain of paperwork he left behind that needed to be sorted through—he'd been a pastor for nearly six decades. Among the files I found a folder that held pages and pages of writings Dad had composed on notepad paper. They were mostly handwritten, although a few entries were typed. It was the first page in the folder that caused me to pause. It read, "Chapter One—Wandering and Wondering." The pages that followed were overflowing with short vignettes that Dad had written over the decades. One entry was dated 1953 while another noted a date in 1997. It was a treasure left for his children to find. We came to the realization that he probably hoped to compile his writings into a book someday. With the help of publisher Debbie Capeci, and the encouragement of Dan Mortensen, the VP of Operations at Woodcrest Villa in Lancaster, our father's collection of wonderings and wanderings is now a reality. It is our hope that the reader will get to know the man that we knew and loved, find joy and connection in

his timeless observations, and even find some compan-
ionship for their own wanderings.

All proceeds raised from the sale of this book will
be donated to his beloved alma mater, Washington &
Jefferson College in Washington, Pennsylvania. 🖋

—Fred Brown

Wondering and Wandering

"I wonder as I wander out under the sky . . . "

So SANG AN UNKNOWN WANDERER of the Appalachians. We are frequently reminded that the Christian is to be a pilgrim. Preachers and poets have enriched our lives with this theme. The beginning lines of the great and beautiful Welsh hymn, "Guide me, O Thou great Jehovah, Pilgrim through this barren land," stirs one's blood and reminds him of this truth. To be a pilgrim, one must be willing to wander; and to be a Christian pilgrim, one must wonder at God's creation, which shows His power, grace, and love.

God's people have always been wanderers. Is it too much to believe that Abraham was wandering and wondering in the fields with his father's flock when God called him "to go to a place . . . even though he did not know where he was going" (Hebrews 11:8)? Moses must have been wondering about the easy life of Egypt that he had left as he wandered with Jethro's flock and "came to Horeb, the mountain of God" (Exodus 3:1).

Because he was wandering and wondering, "the LORD appeared to him in flames of fire from within a bush" (Exodus 3:2). One could continue through the Bible and meet many wanderers who wondered about God and His creation—patriarchs, prophets, Galilean fishermen, Jewish tax collectors, and the ancient apostle on the isle of Patmos.

It is still possible to wander and wonder about God and His creation. It is not necessary to live in the country; it can happen in the city. It is not necessary to be some kind of peripatetic preacher or television spellbinder. It can and does happen in the kitchens and offices, in wheelchairs and hospital beds. It happened to Brother Lawrence amid pots and pans. It surprised Tom Dooley in bloody Vietnam. It can and does happen to anyone who is willing to pause in his wanderings and wonder about the bushes that burn and are yet not consumed. It must be understood that one need not be great, humanly speaking, nor have great aspirations for God to walk with him along some mountain path or lonely Emmaus road. For this is the Lord's doings, not man's. 🖎

Scenes of the Long, Long Ago

ODAY MY MIND WANDERED BACK to the scenes of long, long ago. Mother had died when I was five years old and we all moved in and lived with our grandparents—our father's parents. Grandmother used to sit in her favorite rocking chair and tell stories and sometimes sing songs that she had learned long ago. She would have us join in singing also. One of her favorites was the hymn, "Nearer My God to Thee."

I remember some of the words of one song that she sang all by herself. It made me sad then and still does. As I remember, the words were:

> I wandered today to the hill, Maggie,
> To watch the scene below!
> The creek and the creaking old mill, Maggie,
> As we used to long ago.

Even as I write them now, a dark cloud of sadness descends upon me. Now, just as long, long ago, I am standing on a hill looking down at Elmwood Park and the waters of Stony Creek. Stony Creek! Lem and I walked along its banks, learned to swim in it, played in it, and fished in it. How we fished in it! Day after day, and all day in the summertime, we were fishing or walking along or sitting on its banks. They were the days. But they are gone now, they are no more. And I feel as I suppose Grandmother felt as she sang those mournful words to a sad time. Stony Creek is still there. But now I am old and Lem is no longer here. He is dead. Time and tears blur the scenes now, but cannot erase them. And I wish, oh how I wish I could recapture those times of long, long ago. But that is impossible. And a sadness fills my whole being because of that truth. It is strange how those words of that old song continue to cast a dark shadow over my mind. I guess Grandmother had to deal with them also.

Isn't it strange how we look back on some old days, old times, and old friends, and try to recapture them? But only Star Trek can have time and anti-time and space and anti-space. How are we to deal with time and the impersonal way in which it sweeps away those friendships and times of long, long ago? And the Lord said to me, "The memory of those times and scenes will bring sadness. For that is the nature of my children and their relationships. Any tampering with or disruption of that relationship brings sadness. But will you not be grateful and rejoice that in your wanderings I gave you those times?"

My wanderings have not yet ceased. And though memories of those times still bring sadness, there is

now also the joy that we shared those times, those happy, never-seemed-possible-to-end times. And there is
joy in the knowledge and assurance that the Lord added
scenes to those of long, long ago, and that He continues
to do so each day allotted to us. And now as I wander, I
am not only to add new scenes to those of long ago but
also to give those I meet moments that, in the future,
will bring them both sadness that they are no more and
joy that they once were and that we shared them.

The Lost Christ

SOMETIMES IN OUR WANDERINGS WE encounter a moment of wonder and forget it, overlook it and so lose it forever. Years ago it happened to a poet/organist, who lamented that lost moment of wonder:

> Seated one day at the Organ,
> I was weary and ill at ease,
> And my fingers wandered idly
> Over the noisy keys.
>
> I do not know what I was playing,
> Or what I was dreaming then;
> But I struck one chord of music,
> Like the sound of a great Amen.
>
> . . . .
>
> I have sought but I seek it vainly,
> That one lost chord divine,
> Which came from the soul of the Organ
> And entered into mine.[1]

Moses paused in his wanderings at the wonder of a burning bush, and Israel and we are the better for that. Four Galilean fishermen amazed at the wonder of an unbelievable catch of fish and, moved by the words and magnetism of a Galilean carpenter, left their boats and nets and the Christian Church was born.

How many, many times the Lord Jesus has surprised us in our wanderings! The cry of a child, the beauty and wonder of a sunset! A word spoken, the Word read or heard! A quiet walk beside a singing stream or the tired and weary face of a woman caught in the rush and roar of a commuter subway! God was speaking to us and we did not hear because we were too busy, too tired, and too eager to get on with what we call living. But is it life?

(I had to pause here for lunch. Why don't I take time and pause to feed on the Bread of Life, the ever-present Christ who knocks on heart's door to come in and sup with me?)

We have been so busy earning a living that we have forgotten how to live a life. We may live a happy life, but seldom if ever a satisfying life. In our wanderings, we must learn to pause, to capture the moment and make it ours. Jan Struther writes of her Mrs. Miniver: "Enchanted, she put the incident into her pocket for Clem. It jostled, a bright pebble, against several others: she had had a rewarding day. And Clem, . . . would be pretty certain to come back with some good stuff, too. This was the cream of marriage, this nightly turning out of the day's pocketful of memories . . . ."[2]

No "lost chord" there! A mountaintop experience is a waste of time, useless, unless we capture it and place it in our pocket of memories. We shall certainly need it as we trudge through our valleys of despair and decision. God has placed in the world many wonders of His love and presence. We sing,

> This is my Father's world:
> The birds their carols raise,
> The morning light, the lily white,
> Declare their Maker's praise.
> This is my Father's world:
> He shines in all that's fair;
> In the rustling grass, I hear Him pass,
> He speaks to me everywhere.[3]

Are you looking? Are you listening? God wants you to find, to hear, and to claim as your very own, "that one lost chord divine." 🖊

Disappointed at Christmas

IT WAS CHRISTMASES AGO. IT was many years ago. It was during the post-Santa Claus era. I now knew where the presents came from—the coal and candy and orange in the stocking. I could go now directly to the source of the giving of Christmas presents—to my father. I even called on my grandmother's help.

All I wanted was the sled. Not a sled, that is any old sled, The Sled. The Flexible Flyer! It was in the days when Norristown designated certain hills for sledding. Traffic, such as it was, was forbidden on them and across them. Wooden traffic horses were placed in the streets to ensure that only sleds rode down those hills. Basin Street was such a hill, and we lived on the corner of Basin and Locust Streets. One block away was Beech Street, and another block beyond was Elm Street. Great hills for sledding! And they were filled with sledders—the children after school, joined by parents in the evening.

As we approached Christmas and the snows came, I could see myself tearing down those hills on my slick, speedy Flexible Flyer, along with the other fortunate kids who already had The Sled. That year Christmas delayed coming longer than any time in my short memory. Finally it came! It was perfect. We had snow with sleigh bells ringing and sleds zinging down the hills. I opened the doors to the parlor, for it was a parlor with the entrance from the sitting room guarded by pocket doors. There was the tree, beautiful, spectacular with balls and all the other colorful trimmings.

And there under the tree was . . . a sled. Not The Sled, not the Flexible Flyer! But some ordinary, common little thing with a name like Firefly. Disappointed at Christmas? Ah yes, I still remember. A Firefly! Not The Sled! Not the Flexible Flyer! Now many Christmases later, the memory of that Christmas brings a tearful smile. I suppose every Christmas brings disappointment to some children. And I am sure many parents and grandparents are disappointed at Christmas because they are unable to buy and to give that special, long awaited gift.

I wonder how many people were disappointed that first Christmas? Certainly Mary and Joseph were not. Their firstborn had arrived healthy and beautiful. But what about the innkeeper? It is quite possible that Mary, Joseph, and Jesus stayed for a time in one of his rooms after the crowds had returned to their homes. The frightened shepherds were not disappointed because they found the baby as the angels had told them. And they were thankful that first Christmas and praised God. The wise men were not disappointed. They were not disappointed, for their search was ended. They saw the baby Jesus and paid homage and gave Him gifts. I suppose that Herod was disappointed that the King of the Jews was born because he was a pretender king of the Jews. What about the people of Bethlehem, were they thrilled or disappointed at that birth? Certainly after the slaughter of their infants they must have added disappointment to their pain and suffering.

Later in His life, Jesus was rejected. On His cross Pilate had placed there a mocking title, "This is Jesus, the King of the Jews." Evidently many of the Jews were disappointed that first Christmas. They were looking for a king. Jesus came, "a little baby thing."

I wonder if we are still disappointed at Christmas? We, who call ourselves Christians, act that way, don't we?

Photographer or Participant?

SOMETIMES AS WE WANDER OR travel purposefully through life, we come across a scene that we want to capture. We want to store it in our memory, to be able to recall it and savor it again. So we take a picture of it. It used to be with our camera—whether photo, slide, or movie. Now we swing around the camcorder and press the button. And we have it. Whether it be a Mount Rushmore or some other majestic mountain, or Lincoln Memorial or family and friends at the beach.

Recently I was deeply moved by three pictures in a Philadelphia newspaper. They were taken by a news photographer in tumultuous and violent South Africa. The first showed a stopped Mercedes-Benz with both doors open. The driver was part way out of the car with a menacing revolver in one hand. In the back seat, slumped over was a wounded man. Lying on the ground outside the car was a third man. There was a pool of blood by his side. He was dead. They were three white South Africans.

In the second picture, the wounded man from the rear seat was now out of the car, on the ground on his back, with his head and shoulders leaning against the rear wheel. The driver was now out of the car, evidently wounded, lying on the ground. Closer to the photographer, he was reaching out toward the photographer with one pleading hand, asking for help, calling for an ambulance. There was no sign of his revolver. The third man still lay where he was. Dead!

In the third picture, the man against the car now lay collapsed in death. The driver lay on his stomach, his arms now wrapped around his head, as though in despair or prayer. There are now three dead men who but seconds before were alive. A fourth figure is seen at the side. He was a soldier who had just executed the men.

It is a dangerous thing to be a news photographer during a war or violent and bloody times such as the one captured above. Could he have helped? Dare he to have helped? Would he have been the fourth dead man instead of a live, dispassionate news photographer doing his job? Without being judgmental, it did make me wonder.

The late Dr. John A. Mackay, president of Princeton Theological Seminary, used to talk to us students about the balcony view of life. One can sit on the balcony and look down dispassionately on the scene below. There on a hot, dusty, dangerous road of life walked, or stumbled, or crawled by humanity. Some were wounded; some were pleading for help. With fervor and passion Dr. Mackay impressed upon us that we dare not, we must not sit on that balcony. Our place is on that dangerous road, helping the wounded, lifting up the weary, and being a friend and neighbor to our brothers and sisters. We are called to be participants in life and not photographers.

And I thought of that Good Samaritan of that unforgettable parable. He, too, could have passed by on the other side. He, too, could have looked and photographed that wounded traveler. But he could not. He stopped and helped his wounded brother. As we wander or travel through life, how many scenes such as the ones in the Philadelphia newspaper and the Bible have we seen? The urge to be a photographer at such times is strong.

Charles Kuralt, as he wandered "On the Road," captured many memorable scenes and talked with many people. In book and film he shared these scenes with us as only Charles Kuralt could. But we are not Charles Kuralts. We are not photographers. We are called to be participants in life and in company with the Lord Jesus.

> Truly I tell you, whatever you did for one of the least of these brothers and sisters of mine, you did for me (Matthew 25:40). 🖋

Forbidden Fruit

GROWING UP IN NORRISTOWN, A suburb of Philadelphia, had many advantages. Among them was
the fact that most of the homes had back yards in which
were many kinds of fruit trees. And they were always
an inviting and attractive temptation to us young boys.
One such I knew was a large cherry tree, just load-
ed with big, juicy cherries, oxheart cherries we called
them. Adding to the temptation, too, was the neighbor's
garage, which was next to the cherry tree. It was easy
to climb up on the fence and then to the roof of the garage. And then to the cherries. I remember they tasted
better than any bing cherries I have ever bought.

We lived in the north end of the borough line of
Norristown so that it was very easy to walk out into the
country where there were fields, orchards, and vineyards
of the farmers. The apples, pears, and grapes we picked
and ate there were delicious. I remember, as we were
fishing on hot summer days, pulling up young cabbage
plants. We would peel off the outer leaves, revealing
tender, juicy leaves. Holding the plant by the root—it

was like eating a double-dip ice cream cone. It was refreshingly cool.

I am sure the statute of limitations has long since expired for those "lawless" acts. Even though we were careful not to get caught, we never felt like thieves or criminals. Why is it that forbidden fruit always tastes better than that which is purchased or given to you?

As I thought of those "good old days" I remember the story, an old, old story, of a husband and wife and some forbidden fruit. They knew there was a "No Trespassing" sign at that particular fruit tree. It was indeed forbidden fruit. These two humble people saw that the fruit of the tree was good, a delight to the eyes and very much to be desired. So they took and ate some. (Now the original story had it that the woman was the one who enticed the man to eat that fruit, but we would never get away with that version today.) No matter who saw it first, they both ate and enjoyed that forbidden fruit. For a while they did. Then, as the story goes, the owner of the orchard caught them and it cost them their house and home in fines.

I wonder if I remember those old times now because I have had a feeling of guilt for what we did. Why is it that forbidden fruit always seems so delectable and delicious that we feel compelled to take and eat? Why do we feel that the "No Trespassing" sign does not mean me? I wonder, do you suppose that the old husband and wife made us do that? Or was it society's fault? Do you ever wonder about things like that? 🖋

The Church

IN MY WANDERINGS I HAVE come across two churches serving identically peculiar purposes. They are
thousands of miles apart geographically and centuries
apart in terms of their founding and construction.

The first church is on the island of Samar in the
Philippines, in a very small village called Pambujan.
There stands in that village a large Roman Catholic
Church, whose name I never discovered. It is believed
to have been built about 1555 by members of the Fran-
ciscan Order. Its walls are several feet thick, two sides
of which were continued beyond the building to form
a high, thick wall, forming a compound including the
church. There are high window openings but without
glass or any other covering. This permitted birds to fly
in and out of the church. This, no doubt, would have
pleased Francis of Assisi. There was a beautiful altar
with much sterling silver inlay. There were no pews. The
people furnished their own chairs or boxes.

Sometime after our military forces arrived there
during World War II, the Seabees ran electric service
into the church for the first time. Bare, unadorned

electric bulbs furnished light. Then the Seabees painted the exterior of the church white. Since it was the tallest building in the village, it was clearly visible from a great distance, especially from the sea. Our naval ships desiring to enter this port used the church as the fixed point for taking their bearings. This was essential because the channel was narrow and twisting with sandbars close by each side. Using the church in this way, ships of our Navy were able safely to find a haven there.

The second church is in the USA in the village of Jeffersonville in West Norriton Township in Pennsylvania. It is a Presbyterian Church (USA) that was built in 1962, replacing an older church that was destroyed by fire. The interior is beautiful with excellent lighting, pews and communion table, pulpit and lectern. There are also lighted stained glass windows. The church has a high white steeple, clearly the highest point in the community.

About one half mile away is the Jeffersonville Golf Club, a public golf course. The sixth hole on the course is what is called a dogleg hole. That is, rather than being straight from tee to green it has an abrupt turn to the right. A good tee shot for most golfers (or those who play golf) puts them up at the bend in the hole. The green lies about 200 yards down at the bottom of the hill. It is what is termed a "blind shot," meaning you cannot see the green or the flag stick marking the position of the hole. Until 1962 this was indeed a blind shot. Now, however, all one needs to do is aim and hit

for the Presbyterian Church steeple in the distance.
That is the correct direction.

Thus these two churches, so far apart geographically
and chronologically, so different in their appearances,
serve very well in helping ships and people to move in
the right direction and to find safety and satisfaction.
And the Christian Church has for centuries been doing
just this wherever she has been located. She has nur-
tured us as children and has served us as a beacon of
hope when we were hopeless and a safe haven when we
were lost. ✐

A Wandering People

The Hebrew people were a nomadic people, a wandering people. Abraham went out, he knew not where, to the land that God would show him. He was the first of the wandering Jews. Isaac and Jacob followed in his footsteps. In their wandering, they experienced a dual sense of wonder for God—wondering about His plans for them while also being awed by His presence in creation.

Was it not as Moses wandered that he came upon the burning bush that consumed him with wonder? Did not Moses and his people wander for forty years in the wilderness—murmuring against God, yet wondering about the manner of God? Only when the Jews demanded of Samuel a king, that they might be like other people, did they stop wandering and build and live in cities and villages. They became a settled people and settled God in an ark and later in a beautiful temple. Now that they knew where God was safely domiciled and where they lived, they ceased to wonder about God. Then they were in danger of losing their sense of peculiar identity and divine mission.

It was the task of the prophets of Israel to remind their people that God did not dwell in temples made with human hands. They called them back to the Lord and told them it did no good to cry, "The Temple, the Temple," and forget about God whom they were to worship in the Temple and serve and obey in their living. Even though settled in cities, their wandering and wondering was not to cease. God was still calling and beckoning His people to follow Him, to learn of Him. Can any person ever fully understand God? Is there not always more to discover, to know? Is not life always to be a wandering and wondering?

Think of the horizons that have been pushed back in the worlds of science and technology and medicine. Who would have dreamed of organ transplants, and knee and hip replacements? Consider the fact of a doctor holding in his hands your heart and replacing blood vessels and valves and putting a pacemaker in your chest—a battery, as it were, wired to your heart to jump-start it. Or think of electronics—the wonder of computers, chips, and fax machines. Has that astronomer, wandering and wondering in his mind, discovered an as yet unseen new planet? And so many more advances and revelations because some people refused to let their minds and imaginations settle down in some office.

And does not God have new vistas for us to explore? Does He not still call and invite His people to wander in His world and to wonder—Who is He? Where is

He? What are His plans? Remember when God revealed Himself in Jesus of Nazareth some believed and some did not. And that is still true. It is just too wonderful to believe that God would do that for His people. We are now a city people, a settled people. Even in our vacations we do not wander. We follow a map or a "triptik." And we miss so much of God's wonder when we stick to our I-95s.

In terms of God and His world and people, has it all been discovered? Are there no new places or areas to wander and wonder? Have we eaten of that fruit of the forbidden tree and become like God? And if we are like God then there is no need to wander and to be filled with the wonder of God. And if this is true then we have truly died.

There was a man, a wanderer, who lived to climb mountains just because they were there. Hearing of one mountain in a far off land that no one had ever conquered, he decided that he would be the one to reach the top. Having done this he would then retire and climb no more mountains—the thrill and wonder being satisfied. Having made all of the necessary preparations he began the ascent. As he climbed higher and higher he was filled with a sense of awe and wonder such as he had never known before. Rising one morning he looked up and said to himself, "This is it." For there ahead was the summit! Carefully, laboriously he climbed. Reaching the top he was filled with amazement and wonder at the view. Retiring that night he decided to begin the descent the next day after one last look at the scene before him. The next morning as he looked about in wonder, a breeze stirred and the sun broke through and revealed that this wasn't really the top, but a rather small ledge. The breeze and sun removed mist and clouds and revealed more mountain to climb.

So it is with God's people. There is always more to discover, to learn. God's people are a pilgrim people, a wandering tribe. Only as we wander shall we discover the wonder of the world and of this world's Creator. God grant that we shall never be satisfied in this world except in the wandering and wondering with God. ✍

A Quiet Place

EACH YEAR DURING MY ACTIVE ministry we would go "back home" during vacation time for a visit with family and friends. There came a feeling of joy and contentment being back in old familiar surroundings. When our firstborn, a son, was still a little lad, I began visiting the woods where our gang used to play when we were young. On these trips to the woods Ken was always with me. While these places were very familiar to me, they seemed always to be new and inviting to him. Thus it was also with our other children as they became old enough to join in our wanderings.

The first such trip set the tone and style for all the others that followed. We would walk out along the railroad tracks—trying to step from tie to tie, and seeing how long and far we could walk on the rails. Soon we left the tracks and entered the woods. Always there was the search for the old familiar trails. Occasionally we would find and follow one. Usually, however, they had become overgrown with weeds, vines, and trees. Often we walked on new ones tramped out by new generations of explorers or Tarzans. Old trees had fallen and

29

had to be climbed over or under or scrambled around. We would watch and listen for birds and other animals. Always we would come to the "monkey vines," the wild grape that grew on the trees. There we would swing in the air like some modern Tarzan. This was fun. This was new. This was indeed a great time and experience for Ken. For me it aroused slumbering memories.

We would go to the banks of the old Stony Creek and skip stones. Who could make the most skips? We looked for bullfrogs and tadpoles. We even looked for snakes. Back in the woods we tried to find the old clearing where we used to dig sassafras roots, take them to the creek and wash them and then chew on them. But the clearing and the sassafras were no more. There was more fun walking on the fallen trees.

Then there was the first time we tramped the woods that we came upon the stand of evergreens. Nowhere else in the woods were there any evergreens. The fallen needles lay thick and inviting on the ground, so we sat and rested and listened. "This is a quiet spot," said Ken. "This will be our quiet spot." And so it was each year as more of his brothers and sisters joined our annual visit back home. And it was indeed a quiet and restful spot. All agreed and treated it so. No vines on which to swing! No weeds in our way and clutching at us! No fallen trees to block our way or invite us to climb them! No searching for paths or avoiding mud spots! Just quiet and rest!

Soon, too soon, vacation was finished and it was back to work and to school. And it seemed even sooner that the children grew up and there were no more trips to the woods and the quiet spot. I miss those times. I wonder how many quiet times and spots we miss as we search our way through the woods of life. Do we remember them? Do we even search for them? Or are there too many and too inviting monkey vines on which to play? Or is the work of finding our way too demanding? But we need quiet spots. Our souls cry out for quiet spots where they might rest.

And all the while God's quiet spot awaits us. "Come to me, all you who are weary and burdened, and I will give you rest" (Matthew 11:28). We can come to Him in the Bible. But do we take the time to search and to rest there? We can come to Him in prayer. But do we have a room where we can close the door and talk with Him and listen? It has been a long time since I went into the woods and rested in our quiet spot. And I miss that. But God has prepared for us many other quiet spots. We must, however, search for them. Be assured they are there quietly awaiting our coming. Sidney Lanier knew this:

> Into the woods my Master went,
> Clean forspent, forspent . . .
>
> Out of the woods my Master went,
> And He was well content.[4]

"God, Where Are You?"

THE OTHER DAY I WAS wandering around the golf course. While this may be the scenic route, it is not ideal for achieving a good golf score. Be that as it may, I happened to observe contrails in the sky. Indeed there were several that seemed to be holding to a determined and straight line.

One such set of contrails captured my attention and caused me to wonder. These were high in the sky and seemed still to being made, somewhat as the finger on Belshazzar's wall. But unlike that finger nothing was visible to cause this writing in the sky. Neither was any sound heard coming from the sky. I knew, of course, that this writing was made by a plane, even though unseen and unheard.

And I wondered—where was the plane going? Who was at the controls? Who was aboard and what were their plans and hopes? Obviously the plane had a flight plan and a purpose else it would not be there.

And I thought—where is God? What is He doing? What are His plans and purpose for His children and His world? It is true, no one has seen God. So we often wonder or fear or cry out. Where are you, God? What are you doing? Especially what are you doing to help me in this situation? What are you doing about the terrible, frightening and sorrowful conditions in your world? If I could trust my knowledge and common sense to believe there was a plane up there making those contrails, is it asking too much of my faith to believe that God is and that He is "up there" keeping watch above His own?

Indeed the beauty and the immensity of the heavens speak of God's power and glory. "The heavens declare the glory of God; the skies proclaim the work of his hands . . ." (Psalm 19:1). "There is no speech nor language, where their voice is not heard" (Psalm 19:3 KJV). Yet we want to see. We want to hear God speak. And all around me spring was breaking out in a profusion of beauty. The sweet smell of the honeysuckle. The sounds of the birds. All that had appeared such a short time ago to be dead is now alive with the beautiful, invigorating, and inspiring new green of spring.

Where is God? Where is that plane that made those contrails? I knew it had to be up there. How else explain the contrails? I believe God is "up there." How else explain the wonder, the beauty of this world? How else explain Albert Schweitzer and Mother Theresa? How else explain the Church? And what will you do with the Bible? Explain it as myth or legends? Honest, critical biblical study does not permit that. But, above all, what will you do with Jesus of Nazareth, the Christ of God, the Son of God? How explain His life, His words, His healings, His miracles, His resurrection and living presence?

Mere solitary contrails in the sky? That's all? I cannot accept that. I knew there had to be an unseen and unheard plane up in that sky. I believe God is working His purpose out as year succeeds year. I know that my Redeemer lives. And I know God is and God cares. 🖋

The Land's Promise

THERE WAS A CERTAIN CHURCH which had a very small sanctuary—just six pews on either side of a center aisle. On the rear wall of the sanctuary had been painted one of the great promises of our Lord Jesus—"Surely I am with you always" (Matthew 28:20). Many worshippers as they turned to leave at the close of the service were comforted by this benediction of the Lord.

The time came when increasing membership and attendance required major renovations to the church building. This resulted in a much larger sanctuary with the addition of a coat room on either side of the aisle at the rear. The new wall erected to do this closed off the original wall with the Bible quotation on it.

Several years later a young member remarked to the pastor how much he appreciated that Scripture promise and expressed his regret that it had been painted over and removed. "Oh," said the pastor, "That message is still on that old wall. It is just hidden from view by the new wall." He then took the young man and climbed up with him into the space over the coat rooms and showed him the old wall. There he saw that old promise was still there, "Surely I am with you always."

Life is like that, isn't it? We build walls between the Lord and ourselves. In so doing we remove ourselves from those reminders of the Lord's promises and His desire and ability to keep them. We build walls of work and play that come between the Lord and us. We build walls of doubt and indifference and forget about His promises. We even build walls within the Church that hide His promises and presence from us. Walls of programs and budgets, of power and prestige, of cliques and color!

Trust the promise, the eternal and everlasting promise still stands. Though we build walls, and though we question as did that young man but an echo of the cry of the Psalmist, "Has his promise failed for all time?" (Psalm 77:8). The Lord's promises stand as true today as when they were given. We have eyes to see, but we do not see. Seed time and harvest have not failed. Though the righteous suffer, the evil does not forever prevail. There is the beauty of the flower, the glory of the heavens, the song of the bird, the orderliness of God's laws of nature. We need to hear Solomon stand before the Church as he stood before that old Temple and said, "Praise be to the LORD, who has given rest to his people Israel just as he promised. Not one word has failed of all the good promises he gave through his servant Moses" (1 Kings 8:56).

Often we wander in God's world and we wonder, "Where is God?" It is then that we must remember the promise of the Lord, promises that will encourage and sustain us. Though we come up against a wall that seems to cut us off from God, we must believe and trust in His promises. The writer of the letter to the Hebrews reminds us, "Let us hold unswervingly to the hope we profess, for he who promised is faithful" (Hebrews 10:23). Our hope is that God is and this is His world, just as we pray, "Your kingdom come, your will be done, on earth as it is in heaven" (Matthew 6:10). We must remember, "He has given us new birth into a living hope through the resurrection of Jesus Christ from the dead" (1 Peter 1:3).

"Surely I am with you always," is not just an inscription on a wall, not simply words on a printed page. If this were true, another wall or a closed book could cut us off from this great promise. The Lord Jesus Christ's promise and presence are an eternal truth, a present reality. "For no matter how many promises God has made, they are 'Yes' in Christ" (2 Corinthians 1:20). In our wondering we must remember and believe He is with us. ✐

Look Up

A CHILD SCAMPERS THROUGH THE HOUSE, stumbles and falls over a toy or even a chair. "Why don't you look where you are going?" exclaims the parent. I recall reading about two college professors walking across the campus, and talking as they walked. Suddenly one walked right into a tree, not newly planted. "Didn't you see that tree?" his colleague asked. "Oh yes, I saw it; but I didn't recognize it," was the reply.

There are times when we do not recognize the world in which we walk and wander because we don't look up.

Not looking down might mean that we shall bump into and perhaps fall over the obstacles that clutter life. But not looking up means that we cannot recognize the obstacles for what they really are. There is now much to be gained when, in our wandering, we heed the Psalmist's advice and look up.

When we look up we are able to see the majestic eagle soaring and gliding effortlessly in the sky. And we are reminded that "those who hope in the Lord will renew their strength. They will soar on wings like eagles" (Isaiah 40:31). If we do not look up we shall never see the rosy-fingered dawn and the promise of a new day. Neither shall we see the breathless beauty of the sunset except we look up and be reminded that "God's in his heaven and all's well with the world."

As we wander in God's world and are buffeted by storms, unless we look up we shall never see God's glorious and multi-colored rainbow in the sky. Looking up and seeing the rainbow, we are reminded of God's promise of seed time and harvest. How can we see and feel the mystery and wonder of the heavens—sun, moon, and stars—unless we look up? And with awe we ask, "What is mankind that you are mindful of them?" (Psalm 8:4).

Looking down and round about us we shall most certainly see the evil, the misery and suffering, and the heartaches of this world. When we look down into the grave we are overcome by the presence of death and the feeling of the shortness and uncertainty of life. But when we look up we see the risen Lord and are assured of the gift of eternal life. Looking up we are reminded that in Christ we have overcome death. We have to look down and around us as we walk in and through his world. We have not been promised a life without pain and suffering. We have been promised that we can and shall overcome these obstacles if only we look up. Therefore, as you wander and wonder, look up and be-hold the glory, the majesty, the love and power of God in the world and in our lives. 🖋

Travel Safely

$\mathcal{I}$T HAPPENED IN THE DAYS before automobiles and planes. People then depended upon horses and buggies for the traveling that they did. It seems that this very wealthy woman had lost her driver, for whatever reasons I do not remember. She let it be known that she would be interviewing those who would like to assume this job. Now this was appealing to many because she was known as a fair and generous employer. Many, therefore, were interviewed by her.

Among the questions she asked was one about driving along a certain road at a particularly dangerous spot. It was in the days before there were metal or concrete guardrails along the sides of roads. The edge of that road ended in a precipitous drop of several hundred feet. She asked each applicant how close they could drive safely to that edge. Many who were experienced and skillful drivers and handlers of horses and who had excellent depth and distance perception were quite willing to tell her how close they could come to that dangerous edge of the road. Some spoke in terms of four or five feet and some could come as close as one foot.

But the one who gave her the correct answer and who was hired answered, "I would stay as far away from that side of the road as I could."

Life is like that, isn't it? We travel along taking unnecessary chances. We are sure that we can come real close to that edge without falling over the side. Back then that was a very desirable job. So why not go for it? That fruit in the biblical garden was a delight to the eyes and very desirable. Why not taste one? Ask the alcoholic member of Alcoholics Anonymous why he will not try just a little taste. He knows that is all he needs to go over the edge and keep falling until he reaches the bottom, wherever and whenever that might be.

On the road named "Morality," we like to drive as close to that dangerous edge as we can. And some of us have gone over the side and are falling and are not yet aware of it. We think we are driving safely close to the edge. But are we?

More Than a Prophet

$\mathcal{I}$N RECENT YEARS, THERE HAS been a heavy emphasis on the prophetic aspect of ministry and preaching in our Church. The time of the 1960s with its unrest and divisions among our people contributed to this emphasis. The Vietnam War, of course, provided many opportunities and great impetus for the Church and her preachers to speak in what was described as a prophetic way. While I had and still have reservations about that particular interpretation of prophetic preaching, I am not concerned with that aspect of it at this time. It is time, however, that we remember that the Christian preacher is "more than a prophet."

When our Lord Jesus questions the crowd about their response to John the Baptist, He asked, "What did you go out to see? A prophet? Yes, I tell you, and more than a prophet" (Matthew 11:9). "More than a prophet," the Lord's description of John, is also, I maintain, to be His charge to the Christian preacher. The prophets were indeed the giants of the Old Testament and truly men of God. Their messages and their role must always be remembered and honored. Indeed, the Christian preacher who does not include the prophets' messages in his preaching would be greatly deficient in making known God's Word for His people. But they were of the old covenant and we are of the new covenant.

We need to be reminded of the charge of Jesus, the bearer of the new covenant, to those first ministers of that covenant. Speaking to them of His life and ministry He said, "And you also must testify, for you have been with me from the beginning" (John 15:27). I fear that we, the modern-day ministers of the new covenant, have forgotten that Jesus expects us to be witnesses to Him, His life, death, and resurrection. And because of that neglect on our part, the world does not know Him and the joys of the gospel of the new covenant. It is not the task of the Christian preacher to bring the people to judgment, but to the Lord Jesus Christ. When we attempt to judge the people, they attempt to justify and defend themselves, or, much worse, to ignore us. When we bring the people to Jesus Christ, they sit at His feet and learn of His love and compassion and the new life He offers them. Before Jesus one has no defense. One accepts or rejects.

Remember Andrew? He was more than a prophet. He met Jesus, spent some hours with Him. He first found his brother, Simon, and said to him, " 'We have found the Messiah' (that is, the Christ). And he brought him to Jesus" (John 1:41–42). And in the presence of Jesus, Simon became Peter, the Rock.

Remember Philip! He was more than a prophet. Jesus found him and said, "Follow me." Philip then found Nathanael and told him of Jesus of Nazareth, the promised One of God. "Can anything good come out of Nazareth?" was the response of Nathanael. Philip did not argue with Nathanael or condemn his prejudice as might a modern-day prophet. Philip brought Nathanael to Jesus, and the Lord did the rest. If we can but remember that we are more than prophets and be faithful witnesses to Jesus, the Christ, the world will be saved. And are we not called to save life and not to destroy it? ✍

The Search for Eternal Life

OFTENTIMES THOSE WHO ARE GREATLY concerned about heaven and life after death are considered to be selfish in their Christianity. That is, it is thought that their sole concern is that they be saved, that there will be "glory for me" and "jewels in my crown." And all this with no thought for others in society, in the world. They are accused of being selfish and with no understanding of the social implications in and consequences of the gospel of Jesus Christ.

Sometimes these charges are true. But can anyone really be too concerned about the search for eternal life? About heaven and life after death? I doubt it. In Paul's letter to the Romans, the apostle begins with a strong condemnation of those who were wicked. In the second chapter, at verse 7, he writes, "To those who by persistence in doing good seek glory, honor and immortality, he will give eternal life." Those who seek immortality, God will give eternal life. Let us not, therefore, too quickly condemn all those who show great concern for the next world. Perhaps we, in our own concern for the present realities of life—hunger, sickness, poverty,

war—are losing sight of the "celestial city" and no longer have it as our destination.

Perhaps we are like those who start out on a long
journey but quit after one day's traveling, distracted or
too much attracted by what they see there.

A proper perspective of this world means seeing it
as something temporary with eternal life as the only
permanent thing. Certainly the business world with its
ever-changing way of phasing out old skills and intro-
ducing new ones and new methods should show us the
temporary nature of this world. The computer with new
generation after new generation and constantly evolving
and changing vocabulary reinforces this fact. Birth and
death are constant reminders that this world is temporary and cannot be our goal. If we set our hearts and
minds on the temporal things that pass away, what of
permanence shall we have built? Are we not called to be
pilgrims? Are we not called to "desire a better country,
that is a heavenly one?" With this as our goal, our eyes
firmly fixed on the city "whose builder and maker is
God," we travel through this world as pilgrims . . . and
also as "Good Samaritans"! 🖋

Eternal Life

What will eternal life be like?
What is it like in eternity?
Are there no days, are there no years?

What about Sunday? What will it be?
There is no Sunday, every day is the Lord's Day, you
    see.
Then, will there be no hour of worship?
No. For there are no hours in eternity;
And one worships God with all his being--
Verily with all his heart, soul, strength, and mind.

But surely, there will be Christmas
And Easter, that great day which makes all Christians
    one.
No. Not Christmas nor Easter either.
For then we know Christ was, is, and ever shall be--
For Him there was no beginning.
There is no winter of stillness and death--
No hungering for a bloom, for life,

Which gentle spring brings in her path.
With Christ, all is life and power.
Not new life, but eternal life.
Which changes not with the changeless Christ.

Farewell to the roll of the years,
To the reawakening of the day of sorrow.
Gone is the heartache for the joys gone by.
No more bends in the road ahead.
Just sailing outward and onward
Eternally with the eternal God. 🖋

The Searcher

HE WHO LOOKS AT LIFE as though he has had life's crowning joy or achievement lives at a slackening, dying pace. The athlete who remembers and always looks back to the "grand slam home run," the winning goal, the world's record, or winning the gold is a finished, "over the hill" athlete. For her or him it has happened. For such a one life will tend to atrophy, for each day moves him farther and farther away from that point in time which happened in the past.

Indeed this is an act of futility. No matter how zealously one may seek to retain or to recapture the thrill or joy of a past experience, he will fail. The very attempt to do so is in itself the confirmation of one's failure to hold on to or to find the thrill of that moment in the past. Thus the "born-again Christian" must beware lest he tries to relive the moment or event when Jesus became for him Lord and Savior. The memory remains, of course. And this should be a sweet memory and a lesson from the past and the beginning of a new life.

If, however, one constantly searches for and is on the lookout for life's crowning joy or achievement, each such experience is another happy and joyous step upward, onward, and outward to Christ. Such a one then is growing, his life is a strengthening process, not a weakening position. His life is one of expansion, not of shrinking. (The athlete who thinks his best was in the past will prove it to be true. The athlete who is constantly seeking to learn, to improve his skill will continue to grow and perform better.) The searcher is one who lives eagerly and expectantly, for each moment that lies ahead might be that moment of perfect revealing and fulfillment. He walks with the Lord of life. He knows the Lord is with him and leading him. But he also knows that he sees through a glass dimly. Each day more of the Light shines through the darkness. He knows, he believes that he shall arrive at that perfect Light and finally rejoice in that Presence. ✐

Suffering

On the cross our Lord Jesus cried out, "My God, my God, why have you forsaken me?" (Mark 15:34). Suffering causes us to cry out to God also, doesn't it? We pray, we plead, we confront God with our suffering. Does this change God's mind or attitude toward us and our suffering? I think not. God always loves us, constantly seeks us and our well-being. Jesus reveals to us in His parable of the Prodigal Son a heavenly Father always ready to forgive and to receive us home. He does not cause or rejoice in our suffering. He loves us.

Our suffering can and does change us in body, mind, and spirit. Like the unrepentant thief we can curse God and remain in our suffering. We can become bitter in spirit and close ourselves off from divine as well as human comfort. Suffering can soften us, remove the hardness from our lives and make us more ready to receive God and His love and healing. Suffering can also cause us to look at others and their suffering in a more understanding and compassionate way and so draw us into a more sympathetic relationship with our brothers and sisters. It is not that "misery loves company" but that the sufferer reaches out to and loves and helps the suffering brother and sister. Suffering can also lead us to a deeper understanding and appreciation of the sacrifice and the suffering of Christ for our sakes.

Our suffering can also change the world. Are you not amazed at the amount of suffering some people endure? Their spirits remain calm and bright and their outlook hopeful and cheerful. Again, people are moved as they see the suffering of others. We weep when we see others suffering intense pain. We feel frustrated when we are helpless to ease or remove the suffering of others. Then, too, it is when we observe the quiet way in which some accept and endure suffering that they win us to themselves as friends. The centurion at the crucifixion was won by the suffering Christ on the cross and said, "Surely he was the Son of God" (Mathew 27:54).

Amazed, moved, and won! This is what the quiet and trusting suffering of the Christian can do to the world. Until that day when "at the name of Jesus every knee should bow, in heaven and on earth and under the earth, and every tongue acknowledge that Jesus Christ is Lord, to the glory of God the Father" (Philippians 2:10–11). 🖎

Easter

When Jesus was born on Christmas day,
The world rejoiced with angel songs.
'Twas peace on earth, good will to all
And calendars were changed on the walls.
No more "in the fifteenth year of the reign of Emperor
   Tiberius."
Now it is in the year of our Lord.
Anno Domini.
When Jesus, the Christ, was raised from the dead,
When women searched for Him among the dead,
It was "As it began to dawn" they came
And found the tomb empty; as He had said.
Why look for the living among the dead?
Why turn the pages of calendars still?
When Christ gives us eternity in which to live.
Christmas comes each year with songs.
Easter confirms the angel songs.

Parable

THE WORLD IS THE PARABLE which points to the reality—Deity, God. All creation, all nature declares God's praise. The Psalmist knew this:

> The heavens declare the glory of God; the skies proclaim the work of his hands (Psalm 19:1).

So, too, did the poet know this:

> This is my Father's world,
> And to my listening ears
> All nature sings, and round me rings
> The music of the spheres.[5]

> In the beginning God created the heavens and the earth (Genesis 1:1).

Idolatry, therefore, is the confusing of the parable with the reality. We are too quick to believe that the world is real, and God is unreal—a character from fiction, a figment of the imagination. The world is here. I can see it, hear it, touch it. But where is God? Who has seen God? Who has heard God?

Consider, though, Jesus Christ's use of the common things of the world in His parables. He spoke of seeds and soils, of vines and branches, of vineyards and barns. He took the ordinary things of life to point to the extraordinary reality of the divine Creator and Sustainer of life. To understand and to be blessed by the parables of Jesus, one must look beyond them to the truth of which they are but the vehicles. So it is that, if we have ears to hear and eyes to see, Jesus leads us to see and hear God all about us in the world in which we live. But we must be careful not to identify the world with God and so lose Him.

But then in a very humble and ordinary part of the world, God did merge the parable with reality. Jesus, the Son of God, was born of the virgin Mary in a small province of the Roman empire called Palestine. And in a village called Bethlehem, "small among the clans of Judah" (Micah 5:2)! It was here long ago that the Divine burst into the human, the Divine vertical intersected the human horizontal. And at that point in space and time the real became the parable, and the parable became the real. So great was that act, so meaningful in the history of mankind and the world that all time takes its beginning from that point and all humanity finds its meaning, its destiny, and its God in that child born there. For, "Behold, a virgin shall conceive, and bear a son, and shall call his name Immanuel" (Isaiah 7:14). God with us! ✒

The Gospel in the Snow

THE LATE DR. ANDREW BLACKWOOD, professor
of homiletics at Princeton Theological Seminary,
introduced me to these words about meeting God in the
snow. But the attraction and magic of the snow caught
me many years ago as a young boy. We used to run
through Elmwood Park and walk in the country along
old Stony Creek. We knew where there were swimming
holes and fishing holes and where we had piled stones
in shallow places so that we could cross the creek without getting wet.

A favorite time for those walks was in the winter-
time after a snowfall. There was a mysterious quietness
then. Even our boyish shouts and laughter were quieted.
And everything, everything was so white, so brilliant-
ly, perfectly white. Years later I would remember these
scenes as the beautiful words of the prophet were read,
"Though your sins be as scarlet, they shall be as white
as snow" (Isaiah 1:18). Now the beauty and mystery
of the snow is revealed. In it is seen the love and grace
and forgiveness of God in Jesus Christ. The ugliness
and the blackness of my sinfulness is covered up. God

has covered it up, and now I stand before Him pure as the new fallen snow. This now passes from theology to experience and my heart is gladdened.

And the quietness of the snow reminds me of God's quiet moving among His children.

> How silently, how silently
> The wondrous gift is given.

Quietly God entered the world in Jesus, born in Bethlehem. History affirms that. Now I can personally testify to God's quiet and sure work of forgiveness. We lived one time in a manse just one-and-one-half blocks from the mainline of the Long Island Rail Road. They used steam engines then—noise, clattering through the village. I would awake after a snowfall and there was now a quietness over all my world. The trains could barely be heard. Auto traffic was silenced. The snow reminded me of God's quieting my protestations of confession with His sure mercies and forgiveness. This was not the time for the sound of the trumpet. Quietly, and to each one personally, God comes and blankets our scarlet sinfulness with a blanket of pure snow. ✑

Near to the Heart of God

I HAVE JOINED WITH OTHERS IN singing:

> There is a place of quiet rest
> Near to the heart of God.[6]

And I have wondered about that place as I have wandered in my living and in my thoughts.

That there is such a place is confirmed by the lives and testimonies of countless Christians who have wandered this earth before us. But for us the question is where is this place and how do we get there?

A scientist wrote that he was disturbed by those who spoke and acted as though they were on intimate terms with the Almighty. He was referring to those who display a cocksure, old buddy, pals-y attitude to and relationship with God. They know all the answers, for God has enlisted on their side. I am not sure that they have found that "place of quiet rest," for oftentimes they are caught up in a frenzy of activity or surround and insulate themselves in a blanket of pious phrases and poor platitudes.

Those who find this place do not exhibit this intimate and close feeling toward God about which the scientist complained. Though they are indeed close to God, they are overwhelmed with the feelings expressed by the prophet and the apostle. Said Isaiah when he saw the Lord, "Woe is me! for I am undone; because I am a man of unclean lips . . . for mine eyes have seen the King, the LORD of hosts" (Isaiah 6:5 KJV). His closeness to God served but to make him more aware of the vast gulf of difference between him and the Lord. Peter, in a rare moment of insight and inspiration, turned to the Lord Jesus and cried out, "Depart from me; for I am a sinful man, O Lord" (Luke 5:8). Coming close to the Lord, Peter was made acutely and painfully aware of the difference between him, a sinful man, and Jesus Christ, the sinless God-man.

Is it not true that the closer we come to Jesus the farther from Him we feel we are? Our soul, our life, is laid bare in all its weakness and sinfulness in the presence of the Perfect Man. Though we feel this distance, Jesus overcomes that feeling and holds us close. He is nearer than breath and life itself. This genuine closeness, however, does not breed familiarity, but humility and love. Thus God, in Jesus Christ, reconciles us to Himself, and in this reconciliation, this closeness to God, we are filled with gratitude and joy and peace.

Thus as we wander we are never far from the love of God in Jesus Christ. And our hearts sing for joy:

> O Jesus, blest Redeemer,
> Sent from the heart of God,
> Hold us, who wait before thee,
> Near to the heart of God.[7]

In His World

IT WAS WITH JOY AND youthful abandon that we walked across the fields and along the banks of Stony Creek. The snow lay before us, deep and crisp and even. We were the first to make the tracks in the snow, explorers, first to leave "footprints on the sands of time." But this sand was snow.

But we were not the first. There before us were marks of births. The small, barely seen marks of the sparrows! Chasing them away were the deeper and larger trackings of the crows. Looking about we could see the indentations made by "brer rabbit" as he had hopped along his erratic way. On the banks of the creek we saw the prints of the feet of the muskrat, as he looked for his old sliding-board spot on the bank. And he left a trail so he could retrace his steps home—not of bread crumbs or a string, but the clear, straight mark of his tail.

We were not the first to walk there. Man never is the first to walk anywhere in God's creation, even on the moon. The Creator was there first. And He still walks there before us, and with us if we but look.

My mind and memory are flooded with the names and faces of parents and grandparents, and family; of teachers and pastors and Sunday School teachers; of friends. All of these helped to open my eyes to see that God still walks in His world. They were in Christ, and Christ was in them. And I was blessed to see the footprints of God in His world. The healing touch of doctors and nurses reminded me of the presence of the Divine Physician. A young man dives into the ice-filled waters of the Potomac to save a young woman and tears fill my eyes with the wonder of God's love and sacrifice. "And they shall call his name Emmanuel, which being interpreted is, God with us" (Matthew 1:23). And He will never leave His world. Christmas and the snows of Christmases past remind me of that. ✐

Lessons Learned Wandering on a Golf Course

*F*IRST YOU MUST LEARN THE difference between a "golfer" and one who plays golf. People who know me know that I spend too much time on the golf course. Frequently one will say, "Oh, you're a golfer." Always, always, my response is, "No, I am not a golfer. Arnold Palmer and Jack Nicklaus are golfers. I play golf." The difference is measured first in ability and then in finances. I pay to play. They play and get paid.

I usually play early in the morning. The group I play with is almost always the first off the tee. The result is the grass is usually wet and glistening like a mirror off the rays of the low-in-the-sky sun. When we hit into the sun this causes a problem. We are walking into a bright sun, looking for a small, white, wet ball nestled demurely and skillfully in the wet grass. (This is sometime the only advantage a wanderer such as I am has. It is sometimes easier to find a ball in the rough than in the fairway.) As we wander and look, it is often better to walk backwards, with your back to the sun and then look back. Oftentimes we discover that as we walked into the sun we walked right past the ball (quite frequently between the wheels of the pull golf cart without seeing it). Looking back we could see and find our golf balls.

Life is like that very often. The Hebrew festivals of Passover, Hanukkah, and Purim are reminders to look back and see, discover again how God delivered the people from bondage and death. And then take heart, trust God. Indeed the Bible is full of instances when the people were urged to look back, to remember. The Christian festivals of Christmas and Easter are invitations to look back and to remember. Remember that about two thousand years ago in Bethlehem of Judea a baby was born. Name him Jesus—remember He has come to save, to redeem people from the bondage of sin. Remember, "is born this day . . . a Savior, who is Christ the Lord"—that is the promised Messiah. Remember, "they shall call his name Emmanuel," God with us. Remember, God came to earth in human form, a man to show us God's love and way and truth and life. Look back and see three crosses on a hill outside Jerusalem, and on the cross in the middle this Jesus, the Christ, the God-man dying for the sins of mankind, offering by His life and death redemption, forgiveness, and eternal life. Look back and see and remember the stone was rolled away, the tomb was empty and Jesus, the Christ, was alive. Sin and death were conquered. As we wander through life we must look back and remember lest we cut ourselves off from our roots and become as people without a country; we're called to be pilgrims not lost wanderers.

I remember also hitting that errant golf ball out of bounds, into the trees and rough. Yes, and also into sand traps called bunkers. But I cannot cry out, "The devil made me do it." No, I did it, I hit it there. And there came to my mind the times I failed the Lord and family and neighbors and tried to excuse myself. But it did not work. It does not work, neither on the golf course nor in life. Honest confession in life, confession of a bad swing on a golf course—this is the only way to a better life and a better game of golf. And those sand traps! What a place to lose your religion and blame a bad bounce or bad luck. And sometimes in the sand traps of life we want to blame God and so excuse ourselves. But God does not build sand traps—neither on the golf course nor in life.

Finally, it is so easy, so enticing to look up and to see where the ball is going. And, to one's dismay, you usually do see where it goes. But the idea is to strike the ball, to concentrate on it and strike it correctly. When you do this (I have been told) the ball is more apt to go where you want it to go. The best way, the only way to wander along life's way is to concentrate on the Lord—to watch for and to listen to Him. Trust the destination and the arrival to Him. Look back and remember. ✍

Wandering Into the Unknown

MANY, MANY YEARS AGO, WE decided to follow one of the branches of Stony Creek to see where it would go and from whence it came. We knew all about Stony Creek from Sterigere Street in Norristown, through Elmwood Park and one branch that ran west and into Norristown State Hospital property. There was another branch that ran north through Coul's Farm, past Brush's property and along the path of the old P & W rail line. We had set traps for muskrats there, but had never gone beyond Germantown Pike.

This day we decided to wander along the creek and into unknown territory. We continued until we came to a highway and realized it was DeKalb Pike, the present Route 202. We were at the bottom of the hill that leads up to the William Penn Inn at Sumneytown Pike. We had wandered far enough, had seen enough and decided to begin the walk home to the north end of Norristown.

I am sure that you have done some wandering and exploring—by train, plane, car, or RV. You have probably visited strange and, until then, unknown places. In all probability you started out with plans, maps, tour guides, and tips from friends who had been there before. There are preparations to be made, packing of clothing, cameras, and camcorders. There is a feeling of happy anticipation, and wonder about the trip and the destination. But we do get ready and leave, don't we?

What about when the time comes to "shuffle off this mortal coil" and wander into the unknown? What then? How do we face it? What preparations shall we make? We have become accustomed to our astronauts wandering off into space and, by the magic of radio and television, wandering with them. But we know they will come home again. What about when the time for "lift off" comes and we must wander off beyond space stations, stars, planets, and galaxies? Into the unknown from whence no mortal has ever returned!

There is a way. There is One who has been there and has returned. Jesus of Nazareth, the Christ, the Promised One of God. Born in Bethlehem of Judea. He was sent to the world by God. Jesus is the way to the unknown, the truth about the unknown, and the life that destroyed the power of sin and death and lives forever. As we wander ever closer to the unknown, Jesus reminds us, "Do not be afraid. I am the First and the Last. I am the Living One; I was dead, and now look, I am alive for ever and ever!" (Revelation 1:17). Do you wonder about this? Remember Martha as she came weeping to Him because her brother, Lazarus, had wandered off into the unknown, "Lord if you had been here, my brother would not have died" (John 11:32). Remember also the words of assurance of Jesus in verse 25, "I am the resurrection and the life. The one who believes in me will live, even though they die."

When we travel around this country or the world, we call ahead and make reservations with some motel or hotel. That is the wise thing to do. Jesus has gone into the unknown place we call heaven. He has made a reservation for you there. This is your confirmation, "And if I go and prepare a place for you, I will come back and take you to be with me that you also may be where I am" (John 14:3).

In all our wandering, that is the wonder of it all. ✒

Born Again

WE ARE MADE IN THE "image and likeness of God"—that is God is in us. The kingdom, Jesus says, is within you, among you. That is to say that when we accept Jesus as the Lord of our life and permit Him to rule over our desires, thoughts, and actions, then God (the kingdom) is within us. Our sinfulness destroys this image and likeness and, in a sense, subverts, perverts, or defaces our very beings. Just as Jesus, the Christ, was cast out of Nazareth and Jerusalem, so we cast or drive God out of our lives; and we declare ourselves to be no longer His. "His blood be upon us," we arrogantly and sinfully cry out.

Jesus, the Christ, has come to woo us and to win us back to God—to His image and likeness. We are to love one another as Christ loves us. We are to keep His commandments and so to abide in His love. And thus, as the branch abides in the vine and derives its life from the vine, we shall derive our life (image and likeness to God) from this abiding relationship to Jesus, the Christ. Truly Jesus has come that we might be "born again," to be born from above (by the power of God in Jesus, the Christ), to be recreated in the image and likeness of God. We become His and are no longer under the guilt and power of sin.

When we are "crucified with Christ," the old man, that is the defaced image, is destroyed. When we rise with Him we rise a new creature, different from the old sinner. "Therefore if any man be in Christ, he is a new creature" (2 Corinthians 5:17 KJV). Oh! to abide in Christ, in His love, in His commandments. For here and here only is life, life for which we have been created and for which our spirits yearn.

Waiting for the Child

THE FOLLOWING ARE TWO TRUE stories that illustrate
the truth, "What a difference a birth makes."

It came to pass in the year of our Lord 1945, that
a decree went out from the Secretary of the Navy in
Washington, DC, that all the sailors in the US Navy
were to count their "points" to see when they could be
separated from the Navy and at long last return to their
homes and their loved ones. The war (World War II)
was over and sailors accumulated points by such means
as months in service, battles engaged in, etc. Another
immediate way of separation was if you were the father
of four children.

And all the sailors began counting points and
checking them with the list posted in the ship's office by
the chief. Now on the aircraft carrier Sitkoh Bay was a
sailor named "Tex" who was the father of three children
and his wife was expecting any day their fourth child.
Separation! Deliverance! Redemption!

Late in December the Sitkoh Bay put into a little atoll in the Pacific Ocean named Eniwetok. Some
months before the chaplain had secured some boxes of

Christmas decorations, including artificial Christmas trees, at Pearl Harbor. On the day before Christmas, December 24th, the chaplain, helped by many sailors, was setting up and decorating one of the Christmas trees on the forward elevator that had been lowered to the hanger deck level. In the midst of all this happiness, there came a sound from heaven. Mail call sounded over the PA system. The sailors all hurried off, like the Christmas shepherds in the fields to Bethlehem, to see what was come to pass in the mail for them.

The chaplain was all alone with the Christmas tree and memories of merrier Christmases and hopes of more to come. Then he saw Tex, walking slowly toward him with head lowered. With tears in his eye, he told the chaplain there was no mail for him, no "good tidings of great joy," only a great, overwhelming sadness, a feeling of intense loneliness, and an unspoken fear of what had happened to the baby and mother.

The second story, Luke 2:1–20:

> And it came to pass in those days, that there went out a decree from Caesar Augustus that all the world should be taxed. (And this taxing was first made when Cyrenius was governor of Syria.) And all went to be taxed, every one into his own city. And Joseph also went up from Galilee, out of the city of Nazareth, into Judaea, unto the city of David, which is called Bethlehem; (because he was of the house and lineage of David:) To be

taxed with Mary his espoused wife, being great
with child. And so it was, that, while they were
there, the days were accomplished that she should
be delivered. And she brought forth her firstborn
son, and wrapped him in swaddling clothes, and
laid him in a manger; because there was no room
for them in the inn. And there were in the same
country shepherds abiding in the field, keeping
watch over their flock by night. And, lo, the angel
of the Lord came upon them, and the glory of the
Lord shone round about them: and they were sore
afraid. And the angel said unto them, Fear not:
for, behold, I bring you good tidings of great joy,
which shall be to all people. For unto you is born
this day in the city of David a Saviour, which is
Christ the Lord. And this shall be a sign unto
you; Ye shall find the babe wrapped in swaddling
clothes, lying in a manger. And suddenly there
was with the angel a multitude of the heavenly
host praising God, and saying, Glory to God in
the highest, and on earth peace, good will toward
men. And it came to pass, as the angels were
gone away from them into heaven, the shepherds
said one to another, Let us now go even unto
Bethlehem, and see this thing which is come to
pass, which the Lord hath made known unto
us. And they came with haste, and found Mary,
and Joseph, and the babe lying in a manger. And
when they had seen it, they made known abroad

the saying which was told them concerning this
child. And all they that heard it wondered at those
things which were told them by the shepherds.
But Mary kept all these things, and pondered
them in her heart. And the shepherds returned,
glorifying and praising God for all the things that
they had heard and seen, as it was told unto them.

What a difference a birth makes.
What a difference that birth has made.

The Night Before Christmas

THE NIGHT BEFORE CHRISTMAS IS a busy one for the minister. He leads in the Christmas Eve service or services of worship. There are the friendly and happy "Merry Christmas" greetings of the departing worshippers. And often times he is left alone to put out the lights and lock the doors. And to wonder!

Everywhere? Everywhere? Christmas tonight?
I fear not. For there are those
Who, bending 'neath "life's crushing load,"
Do not hear the angels' song, of peace on earth, good
    will to men.
Their ears stopped by the world's harsh din,
And their hearts burdened with the hurt of sin.

Joy to the world? The Lord is come?
Yes, but there are many who know it not.
They have been so busy coming and going,
So frantic in their haste of getting,
They have missed the good news of heaven's coming,

To touch the earth with joy and gladness
And at their latched doors true joy still waits.

There's a song in the air?
There's a roar of jet engines as planes dive and bomb
And people huddle in cellars and stables
And shake with each crash as bombs,
And guns sing their song of death.
A frightened mother holds close to her breast
The baby who stirs and gives a low cry.

The night was silent, and all was calm,
Centuries ago when Christ was born.
The shepherds left their flocks that night,
Urged on by the angel chorus on high,
To find in Bethlehem Mary's firstborn Son.
And still Christ is found by all
Who come to Bethlehem town.

Everywhere? Everywhere? Christmas tonight?
Yes, everywhere for the Lord is come,
With tidings of joy for everyone.
The herald angels sang it first,
Now we are the singers of the Lord's birth.
Joy to the world, the Lord is come:
Everywhere, everywhere, Christmas tonight. 🖋

The Moral Law

You have heard that it was said to the people long
ago, "You shall not murder, and anyone who mur-
ders will be subject to judgment." But I tell you
that anyone who is angry with a brother or sister
will be subject to judgment. Again, anyone who
says to a brother or sister, "Raca," is answerable
to the court. And anyone who says, "You fool!"
will be in danger of the fire of hell. Therefore, if
you are offering your gift at the altar and there
remember that your brother or sister has something against you, leave your gift there in front of
the altar. First go and be reconciled to them; then
come and offer your gift (Matthew 5:21–24).

Is JESUS HERE SAYING THAT when we are guilty of
these and similar actions God will punish us—even
to sending us to hell? In other words, is God sitting as a
judge and judges (condemns) us for these infractions of
His law?

I think not. Rather, God has established laws of human conduct, moral laws dealing with our relationship to self, others, and God. Just as He has given us an orderly and trustworthy universe—i.e., there are fixed and immutable laws of nature, physics, chemistry, etc. We use these laws to our advantage. That is, we live by these laws. Therefore we use aerodynamic laws to allow us to control the law of gravitation. In the same manner the law of gravitation enables us to fly safely without fear of being pulled out of the protective envelope surrounding the earth and hurtling out into the limitlessness and boundlessness of space. When we disregard or break these universal laws we do so at our own peril. By this, I mean that the breaking of the law carries with it a judgment and penalty. For example, ignore the law of gravity by stepping off the balcony of a tenth floor apartment and you fall to your death. Then and there! Instantly!

Just so God's moral laws operate in this universe. We may have difficulty discerning, describing, and understanding them; but they are just as fixed and immutable as those other laws that hold God's universe together. These moral laws are meant to bind God's people together and to Him in harmony. When, therefore, we break one of these moral laws, God does not, as some referee, blow the whistle, call a foul on us and administer the proper punishment. In other words, God is not eternally sitting and watching as some judge and declaring us guilty of some moral infraction and then administering some punishment, or reserving it for a later date—as for example at the time of our death. (This brings into focus our understanding of sin, sinning, sinfulness, etc.) Man's basic and tragic flaw is his sinfulness, out of which flows his predilection to sinning, and from which he needs to be ransomed, redeemed, saved. This happens when man sees and feels God's love in Jesus Christ on the cross and responds in love and repentance. Then begins the real struggle over temptation and sinning which Paul describes in Romans 7 (especially Romans 7:16–25). The cross redeems man and saves him from the curse (judgment) of his sinfulness. It was the realization of this that so moved Paul that he cried out, "Thanks be to God, who delivers me through Jesus Christ our Lord!" (Romans 7:25).

But back to the moral law and the consequences of breaking it. If God does not punch into His computer each day every instance of our breaking His moral law and administer then, or at some later date, His prescribed punishment, what then about our sinning—for such it is when we break this moral law? Is it not this? This law was established for our well-being and happiness and concord. Keeping it, observing it, brings with it these blessings. On the other hand, to break this law, however great or small the particular law may appear to us to be, we do so at our own peril. The breaking or the ignoring of the law of gravitation brings immediate injury and/or death. The breaking of God's moral law brings immediate consequences. For example, when we hate we become hateful; when we lie, we become a liar (not trusted by others and eventually not even by self); when we become bitter, bitterness enters, takes over, and sours our heart and disposition. It is obvious that some moral laws and the consequences entailed in the breaking of them are easier to discern than others. (Is this not true, at least to a degree, of the laws that hold the universe together? For example—air, water, and soil pollution; "progress" and environment protection, the side effects of medicines, etc.) But these consequences are built into all of God's laws including His moral laws. God, through and in His Word, the Bible, and His living Word, Jesus Christ, is constantly reminding us of this and offers the Way, the Truth, and the Life, and pleads with us, "Choose life."

To the Church

You are a giant,
        not just a handsome giant,
        but a beautiful one.
That is why you are always referred to
        as "she," not "he"—you are beautiful.
You are beautiful because you are a bride,
        and all brides are beautiful
        but your beauty is yours because
        you are the Bride of the Lord Jesus.
You are the Bride of the One
        who is most beautiful and strong,
        most handsome and wise.
Yet He is compassionate and loving,
        caring and gentle—
        outstanding of all humanity,
        unique in all creation.
Because He is the Creator,
        who loves you so much.
        He came and died for you—
        giving up His divine life that
        He might give eternal life to you.

Because He loves you and cares about you.
You are a giant,
> but a sleeping giant
> unaware of your strength
> unmindful of your calling,
> and afraid to believe your Lord.

Forgiveness

Have mercy on me, O God, according to your unfailing love; according to your great compassion blot out my transgressions (Psalm 51:1).

*Y*EA, LORD, BLOT THEM OUT. All of them and each one of them. Cleanse me, O God, and forgive me. Yes, God does forgive me and will forgive me. But at what cost! The life of His eternal Son, Jesus Christ. I am Thine, O Christ, Thine alone.

Simply to say, "God forgives," or "God will forgive," is not enough. This is to set too cheap a price on the grace of God. It cost man not one cent, not one minute. But, oh, the cost to God. The eternal God Himself paid the price with His life in Christ on the cross.

When a blotter, a sponge, or a paper towel is used to "blot out" some liquid spilled, it does not brush it aside or erase it. No, it takes it up into itself. So God in Christ, in blotting out our transgressions, took them up to Himself. He bore the sin of the world—yours and mine. Is it any wonder He cried out, "My God, my God, why have you forsaken me?" (Matthew 27:46). 🖋

The Imperative of Love

"AND NOW THESE THREE REMAIN: faith, hope and love. But the greatest of these is love" (1 Corinthians 13:13). Indeed the greatest of all forces, powers, and emotions is love. Love speaks to the lover in the imperative. Do. Come. Love. When you love, you feel this imperative; you feel impelled to do for your beloved—you must. You must speak words of endearment. You must give this gift. You must do this deed.

There is danger, however, of confusing fear for love. All that the lover feels he must do may also be done because of fear. The difference is to be found in the place or source of the power that moves the individual. Fear compels. The source of the power lies outside you and works on you, exerts pressure on you. And so you do because you feel compelled to do. On the other hand, love impels. The source of the power lies within you and becomes a tremendous volcanic-like force within. Thus the lover's heart beats rapidly—his heart well-nigh burst for joy in loving. Such is the inner power and thrust of love.

How can we tell the difference then between love and that kind of fear which often masquerades as love? Can we tell the difference? There are helps.

Are you afraid NOT to do that thing or speak that word? Afraid that you will appear to be less than you think yourself to be? Can that be love? Do you feel compelled by custom, convention, or "it's the thing to do" and so act or speak. Love is oftentimes quite unconventional, seldom counting the cost. There is a kind of magnetic attraction in love, as heart reaches out to heart; and lover and beloved are bound together.

The Wonder of It All

IN HIS PASSIONATE PLEA TO Israel to turn from her idolatrous and evil ways and return to the Lord, Hosea includes these beautiful words from the Lord:

> When Israel was a child, I loved him,
> and out of Egypt I called my son.
> But the more they were called,
> the more they went away from me.
> They sacrificed to the Baals
> and they burned incense to images.
> It was I who taught Ephraim to walk,
> taking them by the arms;
> but they did not realize
> it was I who healed them. (Hosea 11:1–3)

I did not know that it was the Lord who healed me when I was sick. I did not know that it was the Lord who provided for us as we tried to pay our bills and put children through college. I did not know that it was the Lord who put the words in my mind and mouth as I attempted to preach the good news.

I believed and acted as though it all depended on me. What idolatry! The wonder of it all is that the Lord continued to love me, to forgive me, and to take me up in his arms. There is no other explanation for the miracles that surrounded me as I wandered.

Isn't it strange how quickly we cry out to God for help when difficulties or sad times confront us in our wanderings? And how easily we forget God when those times are safely past and the road ahead is pleasant. Not Israel alone, but the whole world, including each one of us, forgets the One who taught us to walk, took us up in His arms and healed us!

It is when one has wandered long and traveled far that they are able to look back and wonder. There are so many times and situations that the mind and memory have captured and videotaped. And as we replay that tape surely there must be a sense of awe and wonder that one was able to come through safely. Even to come through and to be able to look back!

How did I ever do it? How was I able?

"I" didn't. The Lord still says,

> It was I who taught Ephraim to walk,
>   taking them by the arms;
> but they did not realize
>   it was I who healed them.

And so, not "The End," not "The Beginning," but "The Continuing Wandering and Wondering."

Notes

1. Adelaide Ann Proctor, "The Lost Chord," in Coronation Hymns, (Chicago: E. O. Excell, 1913), 61.

2. Jan Struther, *Mrs Miniver,* (New York: Harcourt Brace and Company, 1940).

3. Maltbie D. Babcock, "This Is My Father's World," in The Hymnbook, ed. David Hugh Jones (Richmond: Presbyterian Church in the United States, 1955), 96.

4. Sidney Lanier, "Into the Woods My Master Went," in The Presbyterian Hymnbook, (Richmond: Presbyterian Committee of Publication, 1929), 99.

5. Babcock, "This Is My Father's World," 96.

6. Cleland B. McAfee , "There Is a Place of Quiet Rest," in The Hymnbook, ed. David Hugh Jones (Richmond: Presbyterian Church in the United States, 1955), 271.

7. McAfee, "There Is a Place of Quiet Rest," 271.

About the Author

KENNETH VINCENT BROWN WAS BORN on January 20, 1911, in Norristown, Pennsylvania. Both of his parents were Catholic, and his whole family attended church every Sunday. Throughout his school years, Ken excelled academically. He was actively involved in student council, served as an officer in clubs, played basketball, and ran track.

After graduating from high school in the spring of 1928, Ken started working at McCarter Iron Works and eventually secured a position with the Philadelphia Electric Company. Doubts about Catholicism had begun to concern Ken in his 20s. Following a lengthy conversation with a priest, Ken renounced his Catholicism and joined the First Presbyterian Church in Norristown. After much prayer, he decided to quit his job and enrolled at Washington & Jefferson College. Throughout his time there, he remained committed to Christ and Christianity, sharing his faith with his friends whenever possible. In August 1940, Ken married Anne Pester. He graduated *summa cum laude* from W&J in 1941. Ken spent the next three years at Princeton Theological Seminary, graduating there in 1944.

With World War II raging, Ken enlisted in the Navy as a chaplain and served aboard the USS Sitkoh

Bay in the Pacific Theatre. After the war, Ken returned to Norristown, Pennsylvania, but soon received a call to become the pastor of the First Presbyterian Church of New Hyde Park on Long Island, New York. While on Long Island, Ken and Anne raised five children: Ken Jr., Peggy, Fred, Bob, and Betty.

Ken retired as Pastor Emeritus in 1979 and he and Anne moved back to Norristown. In retirement, Ken served as an interim pastor in several Presbyterian churches in the area. He also enjoyed many rounds of golf in his spare time. ✒

High School graduation, 1928   *Ken in 2008*

At Washington & Jefferson
1937

Ken & Anne
1946

Serving Communion aboard
the USS Sitkoh Bay

First Presbyterian Church
New Hyde Park, NY

Ken at First Presbyterian
Church, New Hyde Park 1965

Ken with his children at First
Presbyterian Church 1961